HOT CROSS BUNS
And Other Old Street Cries

Also by John Langstaff and Nancy Winslow Parker

Oh, A-Hunting We Will Go

Sweetly Sings the Donkey
*Animal Rounds for Children
to Sing or Play on Recorders*

Margaret K. McElderry Books

HOT CROSS BUNS
And Other Old Street Cries

chosen especially for children by

JOHN LANGSTAFF

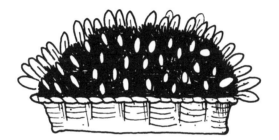

pictures by

NANCY WINSLOW PARKER

A Margaret K. McElderry Book

ATHENEUM   1978   NEW YORK

Music drawn by Philip Bouwsma

Library of Congress Cataloging in Publication Data
Main entry under title:
Hot cross buns, and other old street cries.
"A Margaret K. McElderry book."
SUMMARY: A collection of old English street
cries used by strawberry sellers, knife-grinders,
and others selling their wares.
1. Children's songs. 2. Cries. 3. Folk-
songs, English. [1. Cries. 2. Folk songs,
English. 3. Songs] I. Langstaff, John M.
II. Parker, Nancy Winslow.
M1997.H815 [M1740]   398.8   77-14426
ISBN 0-689-50103-X

INTRODUCTION

CAN YOU IMAGINE A TIME LONG AGO, BEFORE THERE WERE NEWSPAPERS FULL OF advertisements of things for sale, and before radio and television had been invented so there were no commercials telling everyone what to buy? In those days, streets and markets were filled with the cries of people who wanted to sell their wares. They called out about what they had made or grown or about some service they could perform, so that other people would come buy from them or hire them. Some of their calls began to sound like music, perhaps only a chant of two or three notes, while others developed into little songs that people recognized as belonging to the knife grinder, for instance, or the woman who sold strawberries. Most of the time these peddlers were not even aware that they were singing or chanting, just as you are not aware that you actually use two distinct musical notes when you call to someone at a long distance:

(Next time you hear somebody far away calling, see if they don't unknowingly use this same interval of the minor third.)

Street criers caught people's attention with their loud sounds, and a special characteristic call was like a "trademark" for a particular peddler, or for the town watchman who let people know the hours of the night. Many street criers tried to describe their product a little, and some even added a touch of humor for their listeners. Occasionally, a particular peddler would add a bell, a whistle or horn to attract the crowd. We rarely hear street criers today, and most of the cries in this book come from one hundred to three hundred years ago. The idea of calling out your wares to buyers is as old as early history.

You can have fun with street cries in your own way. You can dress up in homemade costumes and find appropriate props to go along with your "business." You can sing the cries back and forth with your friends going up and down a hall in school, or from different rooms or floors. You can make up your own cries about other things to sell, or work you'd like to be hired for. You can use these cries in plays you put on at school, or make up a play in which you can have street criers.

Some of the musical street cries in this book can be sung together at the same time, and I've indicated how they will fit together as part songs. I have also included groups that can be sung together to form "part-songs." Try some of them that way with your friends, using one or two singers for each street cry. After all, in the old days, there must often have been several street criers hawking their wares at the same time in the market.

John Langstaff

GINGERBREAD

Hot spiced gin - ger-bread! Hot spiced gin - ger-bread! Come buy my

gin - ger-bread. Gin - ger-bread, smok - ing hot! Hot spiced gin - ger-bread!

This street cry and the one on the opposite page can be sung together. Both must start simultaneously and maintain a steady beat throughout.

LAMBS TO SELL

Lambs to sell! Young lambs to sell. Lambs to sell! Young lambs to sell. If
(Hot) (cross) (buns) (Hot) (cross) (buns)

I'd as much mo-ney as I've heard tell, I would-n't come here with young lambs to sell.
(One a pen-ny) (two a pen-ny) (Hot) (cross) (buns)

4

HOT CROSS BUNS

See note for Lambs To Sell.

Hot cross buns! - - Hot cross buns! - -

One a pen - ny, two a pen - ny. Hot cross buns! - - -

5

MILK

Will you buy a - ny milk to-day, Ma'am? A-ny milk to-day, Ma'am?

STRAWBERRIES

Ripe straw-ber-ries, ripe! Six-pence a pot-tle. Ripe straw-ber-ries, ripe!

Ripe straw-ber-ries! Ripe straw-ber-ries, ripe!

KNIVES OR SCISSORS TO GRIND

A - ny knives or scis-sors to grind to - day?   I'll do them well, and there's

lit - tle to   pay - - -   A - ny   knives or scis-sors to   grind? - - -

CHERRIES RIPE

Cher-ries ripe, all ripe! Cher-ries ripe, all ripe!

SEVILLE ORANGES

Fine Se - ville o - ran - ges, buy, buy, buy!

BEANS

These three cries can be sung together. All must start together and keep the same tempo.

Dain-ty fine beans, buy my beans. Dain-ty fine beans, buy my beans.

MUTTON PIES

Hot! hot mut-ton pies. Hot! hot mut-ton pies.

CRABS

Crab, crab, buy my crab. Crab, crab, buy my crab.

These three cries can be sung together. All must start together and keep the same tempo.

ROSES, LILIES

Who'll buy my ro-ses? Who'll buy my po-sies? Who'll buy my li-lies, la-dies fair?

OLD CLOTHES

Clothes, clothes, a – ny old clothes? Clothes, clothes, a-ny old clothes?

RIPE PEARS

Taste and try be-fore you buy, fine ripe pears! Taste and try be-fore you buy, fine ripe pears!

PEAS

I have ripe peas-cods, ripe! Peas-cods fine! Peas-cods ripe!

This cry can be sung as a three-part round. Follow one another, beginning where the numbers indicate.

WHITE SAND, GRAY SAND

White sand and gray sand. Who'll buy my gray sand?

Who'll buy my white sand?

A COOPER

A - ny   work for a   coo   -   per?

NEW MUSSELS

New mus - sels, new li - ly white mus - sels!

ROSEMARY AND BAYLEAF

Rose-ma-ry and bay! Will you buy a - ny rose-ma - ry?

A - ny rose-ma - ry and bay? Rose-ma - ry and bay!

WALNUTS

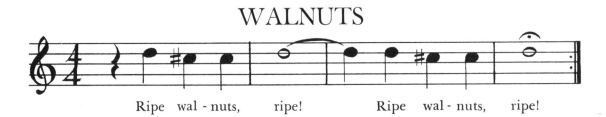

Ripe wal - nuts, ripe! Ripe wal - nuts, ripe!

NEW MACKEREL

These three cries can be sung together. All must start together and keep the same tempo.

Ma - cke - rel, new ma - cke - rel!   Ma - cke-rel, new   ma - cke- rel!

OLD RAGS

Old rags, a - ny   old   rags? Take mo-ney for your rags.   Old   rags?

CHAIRS TO MEND

Chairs to mend, old chairs to mend? Rush or cane bot-tomed old chairs to mend?

BASKETS

All buck - a, buck - a, buy bas - ket!

TURNIPS AND CARROTS

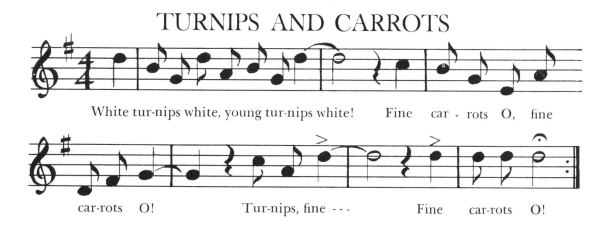

White tur-nips white, young tur-nips white! Fine car - rots O, fine

car-rots O! Tur-nips, fine - - - Fine car-rots O!

THE JUNKMAN

Bot - tles and rags! Bot - tles and rags!

A - ny lum-ber, old iron? A - ny lum-ber, old iron?

NEW OYSTERS

New oy – sters! New Well – fleet oy – sters! New oy – sters!

MATCHES

Do you want a - ny mat - ches? A - ny mat - ches?

SWEET PRIMROSES

Won't you buy my sweet prim - ro - ses, two bun-ches a pen - ny?

THE TOWN BELLMAN

Past three o' - clock and a cold fros-ty morn-ing.

Past three o' - clock; good - mor-row mas-ters all.